MAN UP AND STAND ON YOUR OWN

A short story about dating, relationships, and what it takes to be an Alpha Male around women.

BY
Chris Finley

Introduction

I've met countless guys who have problems dating because they happen to be too nice. These same men often hear from single women that "there are no nice guys out there to date." These same single women will say to their girlfriends, "I would love to meet a nice guy who makes me happy." I have often heard these comments from women (including marriage, several girlfriends, and many years of dating). In that time, I have learned a lot about myself and a lot about how to deal with the opposite sex. It wasn't until 5 years ago (yes, call me a late bloomer) that I realized the majority of my interactions with women have been all wrong. And the times I was successful with some happened by luck" or something along those lines. This may explain my record of failed relationships. Even though I was the type who always had a girlfriend, I still couldn't get the girl I wanted.

It wasn't until I started noticing a pattern in the type of girls I was attracted to that made me start to understand what my problem was. It wasn't that I was too nice or that I was just a guy who was nice enough to get by (that's if I had the time to get used to her). I was just quiet and didn't speak much, maybe a little too laid back when I was in a relationship with them. I realized that I was hiding who I was as a man. I even felt embarrassed if a woman saw me act in an Alpha male way. I thought it was demeaning to her. For example, when talking with a group of men in a room full of people, I would never let myself say how hot a girl was when she passed the group, nor even look at her as if I was attracted to her. I thought I had to be different and stand out from the other men in the group by not exhibiting Alpha male behaviors around women. When a gorgeous woman said to me, "You're so nice," and "You're not like your friends," I would feel very proud of myself and feel that I was doing the right thing by suppressing my Alpha male tendencies. I thought once she saw me as a nice guy, I could show her that all men weren't alike in hopes that my efforts were enough to get the girl and to show the other men in the group how you get the girl. Unfortunately, it never turned out the way I thought it would, and it took me a long time to understand who I am as a man and what it took to get the girl I wanted.

This was when I realized something was wrong. Not with me, but how I viewed women and how I dealt with the women I was interested in. That's why I decided to write this book. To help other men not make the same mistakes I made. I have met many great guys in my lifetime; I have known many guys who can be taken as "Mr. Nice Guys," and I have experienced being seen as a "nice guy" myself. Many nice guys are sometimes called Beta or Omega males.

According to the Urban Dictionary, a Beta male is an unremarkable, careful man who avoids risk and confrontation. Beta males lack the physical presence, charisma, and confidence of the Alpha male. Just like a guy who knew he was losing the girl he just met at the bar to the guy who bought her a drink, but he was too Beta male to do anything about it. The Omega male, on the other hand, is a man who chooses not to have a powerful or important role in a social or professional situation. 'While the Alpha male wants to dominate and the Beta male just wants to get by, the Omega male has either opted out or, if he used to try, given up.

In this book, I will not use the term "nice guy" too often. I will instead use the term Beta male. I am doing this for a reason. I felt that using what seems like a harsh word to most people will help the reader hate the word. If they hate the idea of being labeled a Beta male enough, they will try to separate themselves from what a Beta male is. For all you guys who picked up this book, if you don't learn anything else from this book, remember this: being considered a Beta male is an insult to your manhood; it's just as bad as being called a nice guy.

The Man Up and Stand on Your Own is a brutally honest guide of where many guys have been, where they are now, and even where they are heading regarding the state of their relationship. However, after reading this guide, you are guaranteed to have a clear understanding of how the opposite sex works and why some guys gravitate toward the romantic and sexual companions they do.

Chapter 1

Nice Guy Creation

First off, let's get into how most nice guys (Beta males) were created. When I examined my past as a child and compared it to other beta males I've researched and talked to, I found out that we all seem to have one quality in common: mother.

The mother of a Beta male is highly idealized; she is the woman in this man's life whom he has tried to impress the most, both as a child and as a man. Suppose a Beta male has a father in his life. The father was either not available enough in his life to show him how to be a man, or he was not in his life at all.

For instance, I have a close friend I've known for many years. He grew up in a household with both parents. He is the nicest guy you would ever want to meet. This guy will loan you money even if he hasn't known you for long and cancel appointments to accommodate meeting you. His niceness is sickening.

At first glance, when looking at him, you would think he's a straight-up Alpha male because of the way he carries himself. Of course, looks can be deceiving, but once you start talking to him and getting to know him, all the traits of being a Beta male come out. For example, I have seen very attractive women approach him. I have even seen women ask for his number because they want to get to know him better, but due to his Beta male traits, he turned them down because he wanted to be loyal to the woman he was dating, who had told him several times that she doesn't believe in relationships and doesn't want to get married or have kids.

You may be saying, "What's wrong with that? He's a nice guy dating a girl he respects enough not to see other people around her." A lot is wrong with that because if you're dating someone and there has been no commitment established between you, you're pretty much available to date whoever you want. Since I've known him, he has never had a relationship with the type of woman he's always wanted to be with. The women he has dated or had relationships with were always less than the type of woman he would love to have been with. Because of his "nice guy traits," he got dumped by every woman he loved. If he did have a relationship that lasted longer than six months, the lady was either unattractive, had personal issues, or had some deep-rooted emotional problems that made her incapable of sustaining a relationship for more than a few months.

Often, he would introduce me to the women he was dating, and it would always amaze me when I met the type of women he would allow himself to be with. I would often think that the women he dated couldn't get any worse, but unfortunately, they did. Though I'm not saying that I have the most beautiful woman or that the woman he dates should be drop-dead gorgeous, I believe a man should be with a woman who is attractive to him and compliments his presence.

When a man has minimal self-worth, he will do one or two things. He will either put women on a pedestal or disrespect them. Men like this are so lost that a woman will become their compass. He is so lost that he needs to be with someone more lost than him. The way you treat others is a reflection of the way you treat yourself.

One night while hanging out with my friend at a bar, a beautiful woman walked in, and my friend walked up to her and started a conversation with her. She gave him every opportunity to court her and get to know her. As a result of his Beta male tendencies, he made several mistakes during this encounter. He seemed to turn her off from securing a possible first date. He gave too much information to impress her. He kept bragging about what he does for a living, how much money he earns and how he knew things to show her how smart he was. This was his failed attempt to keep her attention. She would have been more than happy to do all the talking. Believe it or not, women love to brag about themselves, their relationships, and the things they have done. If she is forced to listen to a man she doesn't know, it may lead to her feeling bored.

When you first meet a woman, don't brag , just give her small pieces of information about yourself, make her want to drag it out of you. Most women will never admit that they like a man who is a mystery, especially during the first encounter. Refusing to give out too much information about yourself gives a woman a chance to wonder about you. The second mistake he made was when a bartender (a friend of ours) and I were having a conversation. She started to join in our conversation, giving her input on what we were talking about. My friend felt threatened by this and thought she was losing interest in him, but she was only being herself. My friend made the mistake of intervening in the conversation by interrupting with comments to make himself look good. He tried to take over the discussion within the group, and she noticed this. A woman will see this as a sign of insecurity in a man. His reaction to her getting involved in our conversation should have been different. He should have not allowed it to bother him so he could continue to get to know her better. Even if he was bothered, he should have pretended as if he was not bothered. A woman wants to be with a man who is secure within himself, especially when talking to other men; this shows her you're confident in talking to her and confident in who you are as a man.

Suppose a woman loses interest in you. You don't have to take it personally. Women are like cats; "don't smother them with attention and they will eventually come back around. His third mistake was when she asked where the women's bathroom was. My friend acted like a nice guy (Beta male). He suddenly got up from his seat and then proceeded to escort her to the women's bathroom. This was probably a red flag for her. The mistake he made was being too nice. His action showed that he expected something in return and it came off as being aggressive even though he felt like he was being a gentleman. There wasn't anything wrong in telling her where the bathroom was, but to go to the extreme of escorting her to the bathroom saying, "look at me, I'm so nice, and I will walk you to the bathroom just to show you how different I am from other guys." A week later, I asked him what happened with the woman he met at the bar. He said they talked a couple of times on the phone and planned to meet up sometime, but she never got back to him. My friend's excuse was that the lady seemed like she was looking for a different type of guy. A man should never make an excuse for a woman who doesn't give him a chance to get to know her. However, if you're a Beta male, say to yourself, "it's her loss," and realize where you went wrong and try to correct those bad habits of being a nice guy.

Chapter 2

Beta Beginnings

I was 17 years old when I first experienced being a beta male. It was with my first girlfriend. The funny thing is, I didn't choose her as my girlfriend. She chose me. I was delighted because someone wanted me to be her boyfriend. Luckily for me, she was pretty enough to have my attention, (so I thought). Keep in mind, I was a 17-year-old boy, and it didn't take much to get me excited.

During my relationship with my first girlfriend, I would buy her lunch at school, give her money if she wanted something at the mall (for me, giving her money showed I was the right man and I could take care of her). I even saved up to buy her a cheap diamond ring with the money I got from my part-time job at a fast-food restaurant.

I tried to show my first girlfriend that this is how a man was supposed to treat his woman. I think this is what completed my transformation into a beta male. Her reaction to my treatment started great; she kissed me and gave me hugs. I was flying on cloud nine. During our senior year in High School, we decided to meet at Six-Flags, where I would wear the same shirt and jeans as she had. She wanted us to match, to show how much of a couple we were. I was not too fond of the idea and hated the outfit she had picked out for us. But being a nice guy at age 17, I did what she wanted. That was a mistake because it led to the most embarrassing moment of my young life.

I'm not going to go into detail about the outfit. Let's say, if you've ever seen pictures of the fashions of the late '80s (hot pink shirts and spray paint jeans) then you can picture it. I'm sure you know what I'm talking about. Several hours after being at Six-Flags, hanging out with her, enjoying rides, and playing games, a guy showed up and introduced himself as her cousin. He told my girlfriend that there was an emergency she needed to attend to because one of her family members was in the hospital. Being a nice guy, I told my girlfriend she should go and attend to her family and let me know how things turned out. I went home a little disappointed and concerned. When I saw my girlfriend the next day, she told me everything was fine, and her family member was in good health. I was relieved that she didn't have any issues at home. I asked if we were going to our school prom later that week. She was so happy when I asked her. I had saved all my money so that I could buy a tux and couldn't wait for the prom so that I could show off in front of my friends.

A day before the prom, my girlfriend called me and said she wasn't going to the prom. I was so disappointed. But, being a nice guy, I told her I wasn't going either. You may be wondering, "What's wrong with not going if your girlfriend isn't going?" Nothing really, just that is, if I had been more of an Alpha at the time. I would have gone to the prom regardless and met up with some friends who were expecting me. When I got to school the following Monday morning, all my friends asked why I wasn't at the prom. They told me they saw my girlfriend there with another guy. A year later, after we broke up, I saw her with a guy downtown coming out of a clothing store. It was the same guy who came to pick her up when we were at Six-Flags. Being the nice guy that I was, I never confronted my girlfriend about it. All I knew was that we had two weeks until graduation.

After graduation, she would never speak to me again. My experience with my first girlfriend left me heartbroken. I must have gone through every scenario in my head to figure out where I got it wrong and lost her. In a situation like this, you must accept it and move on with your life. Take it as if it's over between you and her. She's gone.

Though this may be kind of hard to do, if she comes back to you, but ask yourself, "Do I want a woman who left me for another man?" You should never accept a woman who left you for another man for no reason. My first girlfriend didn't see my potential, which meant she was not the right woman for me. It's that simple.

If she dumps you for no reason, then forget about her and fix everything right for yourself. Every time I catch myself thinking about my first girlfriend, I say to myself, "Neediness leaving the body." Don't wallow in your loss. See the little time you spent with her as a motivation to find another woman. Your worth has nothing to do with her approval. There is no dispute about being rejected by the woman you love but don't allow that to impact your self-esteem. Know your values as a man and honor your self-worth. Maintain your dignity by not trying to force a woman to be in your life if she doesn't want to be. The fact is, the right woman will come, and you won't have to prove your worth to her. She will recognize it. Let go of the idea of mending a relationship because she dumped you for another man. Instead, create your own form of closure.

Start a new life outside your former relationship and do what you need to do to move on in life.

Chapter 3

Strike Three

I was in my early 30s when I realized I had a pattern of dating women I didn't want to be with. I was meeting the type of woman I always thought I wanted, but I couldn't keep them long. Eventually, they all noticed how much of a Beta male I was. It was horrible. I would meet an amazing woman who I thought was the one for me, but it would always go the same way in the end. I would start dating them for several weeks. Before I knew it, I was already treating them as a long-term relationship without getting to know them first. I didn't initiate a kiss or hold hands on the first date to show I was interested in them. I was being too passive, thinking I needed a promise or wanted her to make the first move. Eventually, I would get the dreaded Dear John text or phone call.

What they kept saying was, "I like you, and you're a nice guy, but I think we're not compatible." Often, I was so taken by surprise that I would find myself explaining why I'm a good catch, or that they needed to get to know me better. But I eventually learned from those experiences. If a woman decides she doesn't want to be with you, there's nothing you can do unless you have a history with such a woman or some emotional ties. When she ends it, she has most likely made up her mind. However, the beautiful thing about women is that they are allowed to change their minds about you. That's why it's best to say what you have to say to her after she breaks up with you. If she changes her mind, she will let you know.

As a man, you need to move on with your life. If you don't hear from her right away, don't take it personally. She will eventually reach out to you, but if she doesn't, she is not the right one for you; move on to someone else. You need to learn from your mistakes and be aware that there are things you don't need to do in a breakup situation. This will take time and practice. You have to date other women in order to get better in relationships even when things fall apart. When I finally met someone I thought worthy, I screwed up miserably. The relationship lasted only four months. She was the most amazing woman I had ever dated in my life. When I first met her, I thought I had finally made it. I said to myself, "This is the one I was meant to be with." She had all the qualities I was looking for in a woman. She was intelligent, educated, and very attractive, to name only a few of her attributes. When I went out with her, other guys were carried away due to her attractiveness and women-focused their attention in our direction as if we were celebrities.

I felt like an athlete going out with his supermodel girlfriend (Tom Brady and Gisele Bündchen). Ha! That's what I thought. It was so crazy; I had other women staring at me as if they were wondering what she saw in me. We dated for four months before my Beta male tendency started to reveal itself. That's when she broke up with me. After getting dumped, I looked back at where I went wrong and realized where my problem was. I remembered that I had started to display neediness. For instance, when we started dating, she often called me, and I hardly picked up the phone to talk to her initially. As the relationship progressed, the position of power changed, and I started calling her at least once a day. I later realized this wasn't giving her a chance to miss me. I oversaturated my presence with her and gave her too much of my attention and too much information about myself too soon. By doing this,

I was not allowing her to wonder about me. What I didn't realize at the time was that this is a big turn-off for women, especially if they haven't known you long enough.

Over time, she started to act differently around me by being moody and distant. Now that I realized what I did was wrong, I have a better understanding of a woman's psyche. It's so funny how a woman doesn't know what's going on with herself when she's in a bad mood. From my experience and research that I've done about women, I have found that a woman's emotions are so strong. A lot of their decisions are driven mainly by how they feel at the time. All other decisions they make are secondary.

One day, I asked the girl I was dating to come over to my place to hang out. When she came over, she had an attitude and a frown on her face. While we sat on the couch watching TV, my insecurities kicked in. Out of the blue, I told her how I felt about her, and it had only been four months since we started dating. The look on her face became different, and the whole vibe of the room changed. She didn't give a response or acknowledge my comment. She gradually cut our time together short by saying she had some things to take care of and needed to go home. I could tell something had changed between us. She didn't even want me to walk her to the car. That's when I knew the woman I fell head-over-heels for wasn't going to see me again.

A few weeks later, I tried calling and texting her, but her responses were slow to get back to me.

Then one fateful morning, I woke up to a dreaded "Dear John" text. A long text from her explained why we were not a good match due to my Beta male attributes. For example, within the first month of dating her, I was already buying her flowers. And tell her how I felt about her without even getting to know her first.

I was depressed for weeks. I even attempted to win her back by sending flowers and sending her positive text responses. One thing I have learned from that experience was how to deal with women. I discovered that no amount of pleading could change a woman's mind toward being with you unless she wants to. That's why the best thing you can do is to say your piece, such as "sorry to hear that you feel this way. If you change your mind, let me know, It was great meeting you." Cut your losses and lick your wounds. When it comes to a situation like this, you can do nothing to change a woman's mind unless she wants to. You have to let it go and count it as a loss. If she had a high level of interest in you, she would let you know and reach out to you. If not, that means it wasn't meant to be. Move on to the next woman and learn from your mistakes. Since that short-lived relationship, I have gotten better when dealing with new relationships with women I just met.

At this point, I have had several relationships that have lasted for a few years. It has even gotten to the point that it doesn't even bother me if a woman breaks up with me. Yeah, I get a little butt-hurt, but I don't let them know that, and I don't even take it personally. All I'm saying is once you have a better understanding of what a woman is and what drives her, it becomes difficult to blame her if her emotions change toward you. I have learned to look at what I was doing wrong in the relationship and realize a woman is only following her feminine emotions because we (men) have better control of ourselves than they do. Feminine energy it is free-flowing and not bound by rules; it is not restrictive and does not abide by social norms. Intuitive feeling and creativity are commonplace, along with being collaborative and expressive. An example of feminine energy is when a woman wants to find her flow. When dancing she will come up with creative sensual ideas to show her elegance, help a friend with a relationship upset, or trust her intuition.

It's now up to us to manage those emotions that result in a woman enjoying a man's masculinity. The more a woman enjoys a man's masculinity, the more she will enjoy being with him. Always remember a woman's emotion is like the weather. It will continually change. However, learning how to be there for your woman's feelings makes a difference when you are building a long-lasting relationship.

As long as you understand how to cope with her when she's moody or emotionally down, you will become a master of that situation rather than just reflexively reacting. This enables you as a man to be far more empowered in your relationship and give your woman what she needs. This leads to a situation where you two can handle the complexities of relationships and life a lot better. The fact is, science has shown that we (men) feel emotions more intensely than women. Our physical reactions to their emotional feelings are more intense, though the way we handle those feelings tends to be different. We do have more inclinations to hold them in and repress them for various reasons.

Chapter 4

Beta Wake-up Call

It was not until I got into my late 30s that I realized I had a Beta male tendency. Looking back at all my past relationships, there were some things that I did right and some that I got wrong. Often, it all boiled down to the fact that she was the type of woman I wanted to be with. I'm not saying the women I had the pleasure of being in a relationship with weren't attractive, but I believe because of my Beta male tendencies, I wasn't able to secure a relationship with a very attractive woman who would be considered a 10 on the hot-meter scale. For me, they were just good enough to satisfy the inner man in me and able to allow the Alpha male in me to keep them in check. Deep down, I wanted a woman who resembled Paula Patton, Haley Berry, or Scarlett Johansson. You know, the drop-dead gorgeous women that make most men afraid to approach them. Yes, the women I had relationships with were wonderful, and they weren't bad on the eyes. But that wasn't what I wanted.

Sometimes I asked myself, "is this the type of woman I want to be with for the rest of my life, or am I just settling?" Most men settle with women because they know their interaction with women isn't good enough to get the type of woman they want. Instead, they obsess over pictures and fantasize about the kind of women they would like to be with while thinking to themselves, "How the hell does this average-looking Joe Shmoe have that hot girl in his arms?"

I realized several things about how an average-looking guy got a woman who seemed impossibly attractive for a guy like him. First, he had confidence. No matter how the guy dressed—he could have a scruffy beard or not comb his hair—he carried himself as if he was a prize. Secondly, I noticed how he treated her. He treated her like any other person. He didn't put her on a pedestal or treat her as if she was God's gift to men. He treated her as if he had known her for years. I observed this one night at a lounge club with some friends. There was this amazing woman with gorgeous light brown eyes with the most average-looking dude. Yet, he gave her no special treatment nor talked to her as if she were a princess. In return, it seemed as if she appreciated him more by socializing with her as if she was just like any other person.

Women don't like to be put on a pedestal, especially very attractive women. I know this might surprise some guys out there, but it's true. When you put a woman on a pedestal because of her looks, it makes her feel uncomfortable and makes you look creepy and needy. That's why most guys get the "you're so nice," comment from an attractive woman, but subconsciously she says to herself, "I would never go out with a creepy guy like this." That's why you often see a jerk with an attractive woman. This is because a jerk type of guy doesn't validate her. In turn, this forces her to look for validation from him. This is probably a woman's biggest weakness. It is within a woman's nature to look for the approval of others rather than from other men or her girlfriends. A woman wants everyone to like her. They need that validation to make them feel good inside. Making your woman happy and feel good at all times in your relationship is not difficult if you are willing enough to observe and listen to her. The fact is a woman wants to feel valued, respected and appreciated at all times.

Chapter 5

The Psychology of Mannie

Ten years ago, I moved from Boston to Los Angeles for a better job offer. The job required me to go through three years of stressful training for certification in government contracting business dealing with other companies. The classes were sometimes computer-based, while other courses required me to attend meetings or classroom settings. In this one particular class meeting, I was introduced to a guy named Mannie.

Mannie was about average height and somewhat stocky with a smug look on his face. If you don't know this guy, which I didn't at the time, you would take that look like an insult when he looked at you. As we stood around talking after a class had ended, Mannie mentioned that he was working on a big project within the program and couldn't tell me about it. That's when he rubbed me the wrong way. I felt as if this project was so special, why bring it up and not tell the other colleagues and me? As far as I knew, we were all on the same training program. From then on, I didn't like the guy.

A month later, Mannie reached out to me. He wanted to meet for a drink. Since I had only been in Los Angeles for a few months and didn't have many friends, so I agreed to meet up with him to be social. After talking to Mannie, I realized he wasn't a bad guy. He just wasn't good at interacting with other people. He was brilliant, spoke three languages, and had a law degree from Stanford. Mannie's only downfall was his social skills. If you didn't know him, he would come off as smug and egotistical. You'd think he acted as if he thought as if he was better than everyone else in the room. So, I gave him the benefit of the doubt. Since then, I have tried not to judge anybody without getting to know them first.

Several years passed, and I got to know Mannie very well. We ended up becoming good friends. However, I saw a guy who had no idea what being a man was about or how to handle himself around attractive women. His social life was like that of a loser chick-flick movie where things never go right for the guy who always tries, except he had a relationship of three years.

When we went out to meet girls, I noticed he had no loyalty among friends. You know, that unspoken man's code you learned while in high school when you were much younger. He didn't know the code. This told me that Mannie hadn't bonded much with other males while growing up. He was a typical nice guy and would sell his soul if it meant getting attention from an attractive woman, hypothetically speaking. I had never encountered a guy like him before. I have traveled overseas, been in the military, lived in different states, attended college in the south for four years, and then moved to the East Coast. Through those travels, I have bonded with different types of guys in the process. But I have never met a grown-up man in his early thirties who thought the way Mannie thought.

One night, while hanging out with my friend, enjoying a Friday night after-work happy hour at the bar, we met two attractive women. They were having an intense conversation about relationships. They asked us how men and women are different from one another.

During our conversation with the two women, I noticed that anytime I disagreed with them, my friend would side with them, then jokingly respond with, "I'm not with this guy." At first, I was taken back at how he sided with women he didn't know or even agree with. I knew he disagreed with these two women because a few days prior, we had already had the same discussion and he had expressed his true views in our conversation. It was when he sided with those women that I realized my friend was a people pleaser.

People pleasers can be one of the friendliest and most helpful people you know. They never say "no." You can always count on them for a favor. People pleasers spend a great deal of time doing things for other people. My friend would listen politely as the women gave their opinion about men. Even though he disagreed, he pretended to agree with the two women to be liked by the opposite sex. This can cause him to engage in behavior that goes against his values, and women can see right through this. As I observed this from my friend, Mannie, I noticed one of these girls' reactions. Every time my friend sided with their opinion, she would ask my friend, "Aren't you going to support your friend?" Mannie responded with a subtle laugh. That's when I saw both girls' faces; their interest in us diminished.

What my friend didn't realize was that women are very good at reading people. My friend showed no loyalty and came off as a "people pleaser" to them. The two women knew my friend was a beta male who they could control. Their whole interaction with us changed, and they were preparing to leave. When they left, I asked my friend why he changed his opinion. I thought we were on the same page when it came to that subject. He looked at me and got confused, and he didn't know if I was pissed or joking. Then, I explained to him about the guy code. He responded that he never heard of it; said he would try to remember that the next time.

Another night after hanging out at the bar, my friend and I were walking up a narrow sidewalk with construction on one side. An attractive woman walked by us with her head slightly down bundled up inside her coat. It was about 46 degrees. That's pretty cold for LA weather. As we walked by her, I spoke to her, asking how she was doing. She walked at a fast pace and mumbled, "hi." As the woman walked by, my friend started scolding me. He said I should look at a woman's body language before I uttered anything and said the woman looked as if she was about to pull out her pepper spray and call the cops. That's why she didn't speak much. I thought he was joking at first until I looked at his face and discovered that he was serious. So, I told him no woman in her right frame of mind would call the cops because you speak to her. If a woman does, that shows something must be wrong with her. So, I added that she did speak in a subtle voice, but it seemed as if she was in a hurry. If anything, I may have made her day.

According to *Psychology Today* magazine, when you say "Hi" to a stranger, your positivity can make their day. At the same time, you get yourself comfortable talking to attractive women. I could tell that my friend's reaction when I spoke to the women made him very uncomfortable, and the fear he displayed said to me that he puts attractive women on a pedestal and saw them as untouchable human beings.

Another example of his discomfort with attractive women was the night when I was out with him. While we were leaving a night lounge, we saw two gorgeous ladies standing on the sidewalk waiting at the crosswalk for the light to change. One a gorgeous blond and her friend who had long curly brunette hair walked up beside us, eating ice cream. I turned to her and said , with a joking smile, that ice cream looks good. I caught her a little off guard. She responded, in between bites of ice cream, "It's very good. Even delicious." I asked what flavor it was she was eating. "Vanilla mocha," she giggled. We continued chatting as we made our way across the street. I told her to enjoy her ice cream, and she responded, "I will," and we went our separate ways.

My friend's face had turned beet red, and he said that she looked as if she was about to run and call the cops. I responded angrily. "Are you fucking serious? Do you think she was afraid of me in broad daylight walking across the street with many people around us having a small chat about ice cream while crossing the street. What's wrong with you, man?" I yelled. He turned his head and got quiet. I explained to him just because a woman is attractive doesn't mean you can't talk to her. Why would she run because I told her the ice cream looked good?

If she wasn't interested in what I had to say, I'm sure she would have let me know and kept walking. My friends' fear of attractive women frustrated me. It made me realize that his fear of attractive women limited his chance of being with the type of woman he wanted to be with. I could tell from his actions that Mannie didn't see himself as a high-value male and that he didn't see himself as deserving of the type of woman he wants in his life.

Chapter 6

Meeting His Beauty Queen

For happy hour, Mannie and I would usually meet up at a local bar. We would sit and talk while enjoying serval drinks. Having conversation about the politics at work and what's happening in each other's lives.

At the time, my friend had been dealing with family issues. He confessed that his dad was trying to kick him out of the house, insisting that my friend contribute more towards the bills. Mannie said his mom was intervening in the situation between him and his dad. She would argue with his dad about my friend. She said that he should be allowed to stay as long as he wanted or until he was ready.

From what I could tell, it seemed as if my friend's mom had been nurturing him all of these years by not allowing his father to be a father. My friend's father tried to shape him into a man, but his mother interfered every time he tried. This told me two things about my friend. First, my friend's mother ran the household, and second, his father was a Beta male. I advised my friend that it sounded like his father wanted privacy with his wife now that the kids are all grown up, and his dad wanted him to "Man up and move on with his life." My friend gave a big "ah," as if he didn't like what I had to say.

"I wish they would go ahead and get a divorce. I'm tired of all the arguing," he said while pouting.

Soon after, a gorgeous, exotic-looking woman came in and sat near us, closer to my friend's side of the bar. I looked in her direction and then asked her where she was from.

"You don't look as if you're from here," I said. She responded that she was from the Dominican Republic and told us her name.

"How about you?" she asked.

I told her where I came from and then introduced myself. While we talked, my friend interrupted our conversation and spoke Spanish to her. Yes, this guy could speak a second language, just like I said in the previous chapter. He was intelligent enough to learn Spanish even though no one in his family or in his circle of friends was Hispanic, as far as I knew. Being the type of guy he was, he pretty much piggybacked off my conversation. I wasn't upset about the apparent cock-block move. I was more curious about how he would handle this type of woman; the type of woman whom he was not used to conversing with. What I have found when approaching women is that there are no women out of your league; it all boils down to confidence. You have to know what you deserve as a man, and no woman is above approaching and getting to know.

A quote I memorized from reading the book, *The Unchained Man* by Caleb Jones talked about how a man should view himself when being involved with women. "My life and my love of it will always be bigger than any one woman." I believe every man should learn this quote by heart. This one little line has helped me not to get so wrapped up in one woman. I'm able to enjoy myself without looking for a relationship. With this in mind, if a relationship happens, it happens. It's nothing I was hoping for. That's why you should always let it be the woman's decision whether a relationship will come out of your dating or not. Trust me. A woman will always be curious enough to ask what direction the dating is going.

While my friend was conversing with the woman, I was having a deep conversation with the bartender. The bartender was a big, burly guy with a long dark beard and glasses. When the bartender and I talked, we always cracked jokes at ourselves about the stories we told. The woman my friend was talking to was so interested in what we were talking about, she intervened in our conversation, laughing and adding in her jokes. (A slight hint: women love to laugh. It's a great way to loosen a woman up and get her comfortable around you.) My friend began interrupting our conversation to talk over the bartender and me. Every time we said a joke, my friend would follow up with a response, which was very annoying. This was my friend's attempt at getting the woman's attention back on him.

Unbeknownst to Mannie, this behavior showed his insecurities. In a situation like this, a man should never lose his cool and think that you don't have the woman's attention. It is a turn-off to her if you try to overshadow someone else to get her to pay attention to you more. She will lose respect for you. A woman can sense your insecurities a mile away. However, my friend was lucky enough to get her phone number regardless of his lack of confidence. This seldom happens for most beta male types such as my friend. There's a big chance she has a high level of interest in him.

For my friend, you could tell this was nerve-wracking for him. I could see the sweat rolling down his face. My friend excused himself to the bathroom, and when he came back, he was surprised that the woman had not left and was standing at the counter with her back turned, waiting on a slice of pizza to go. My friend walked over to her, to talk some more.

This was a big mistake on my friend's part. He was pretty much depriving himself of the chance of her being interested in him. You always want to leave some mystery about yourself because you want something to talk about when you do go out. In my friend's mind, he was securing his opportunity to see her again. He thought the more he talked to her, the more she would go with him. This thought was wrong. My friend was bringing down her level of interest in him, and what she saw was his insecurity.

Women are very good at reading people. It's one of the self-defense mechanisms that women have by nature. Have you ever heard a woman say that she has a feeling that something isn't right when you're with her? Most women use this sixth sense to weed out potentially ill-suited mates.

Some days later, I met up with my friend after work and had the chance to ask him how it went with the woman he met the other night. Did they go out? He said no, and that they only talked on the phone a few times. When he finally asked her out on a date on the second phone call, she gave him an excuse that she was busy and maybe some other time. When a woman wants to meet with you, even when she is busy, she will find a way to meet you. If she has a high level of interest in you, she will make the time for you. This made me understand that my friend gave too much info about himself on the phone and possibly bragged about his achievements. Women don't like men who brag about themselves to impress them. Believe it or not, women love to talk about themselves. Because I am aware of this, I have learned to speak less on a date. I let the woman do all the talking. Without fail, it works every time. I always get compliments from my dates, telling me that I was the best date they've had in a while.

I could tell by looking at my friend's face that he was disappointed in not getting a date with her. I tried to give him some advice on where he went wrong, but due to his self-centered ego, he put all the blame on her for not recognizing a good suitor when she saw one. As a man, you should never blame others for something that didn't go right for you. First, try to look at where you went wrong. It's easier for people to blame others if something doesn't go their way. It takes the pressure off of admitting you screwed up, and you have to face your mistakes as a man. This was one of my friend's issues. He never wanted to admit what he did was wrong, nor what he could have done right.

Chapter 7

When He Met His Girl

Before I met Mannie, he'd been in a relationship that had lasted three years. He often bragged about his relationship with his ex-girlfriend to other women and to guys as if she was a trophy. I think he wanted to let everyone know that someone wanted him and that he could hold on to a relationship. My friend believed if other women knew he had been in a relationship, they would want him more. Yes, that is true to a certain extent, but women don't like guys who brag, just like I said earlier. At the same time, you have to let women drag information out of you. Never volunteer information unless she asks. Even if she asks, you should be discreet with your personal information. Women are known to take everything you say and break down your response to the simplest terms to use against you negatively. With my friend, he had gotten to the point where he showed photos of his girlfriend to other women. I think this was his way of getting on their good side, showing them he was not a threat. His way of saying, "look, I have a girlfriend,

I'm safe to talk to" when he wanted to get to know them better. Bad move on his part because that automatically put him in the friend zone. On the other hand, Mannie didn't realize that just because he had a girlfriend doesn't mean he had a free pass to talk to any woman and ask for their phone number. That technique is great, but you can't just have any girl as your girlfriend to show off. You need to have the right woman to get another woman's attention and to let her know that you're a good catch. It is good to have an attractive woman to make other women wonder what makes her want to be with you.

Unfortunately, my friend's girlfriend was not attractive, nor was she the type of woman he wanted to be with. He just wanted to be in a relationship. He didn't see himself as a high-value man who deserved the type of woman he truly desired. To put it bluntly, his girlfriend was of average height, overweight, bisexual, and a pot smoker who didn't dress well. She was the complete opposite of what my friend wanted in a woman. She would be considered damaged goods to most guys, and had no desire to be in a committed relationship. This relationship with her was so unique it was surprising, even

46

unexpected, that my friend, who was an educated man, who dressed well, was well-mannered, etc. was with a woman who had no aspirations and didn't want to better herself. The relationship was very unbalanced, which usually caused him to bargain with her about things he didn't really want to negotiate on. This was all done to get her to stay with him; this was all in hopes that she would one day marry him. That's how unrealistic his relationship with her was.

My friend had such low self-esteem that he couldn't see himself with anyone else but her. Don't talk about marriage with a woman or how you want to be together. Don't focus on the relationship; it turns a woman off. Don't lie to yourself and try to perceive yourself as being a catch. "The people we are in relationships with are always a mirror, reflecting our own beliefs, and simultaneously we are mirrors, reflecting their beliefs." — Shakti Gawain.

According to *The Unchained Man* by Caleb Jones, he wrote an article on Mission.org titled, "Why All Relationships Mirror The Relationship You Have With Yourself." He states those with poor relationships have an unhealthy relationship with themselves. They have not found their true identity within themselves but look towards others to define them. He also states that many people gravitate toward partners who are opposites, which leads to conflict. With my friend, this was true. He and his girlfriend were total opposites of each other. My first-time meeting with his girlfriend was when he invited her to join us at our usual spot on Sunday afternoon. When my friend first pointed her out, she appeared from among a group of people standing at the doorway. She was in her early thirties, uniquely dressed, slightly overweight, and used a cane as a walking stick due to her bad back.

At first, I thought it was a joke when he pointed her out to me, considering that I have seen this guy get approached by some very attractive women during my time hang outing with him. If you have ever seen the movie *Shallow Hal* with Jack Black and Gwyneth Paltrow, you'll remember a scene where Gwyneth Paltrow plays an overweight woman and is standing across a field looking to meet up with Hal, played by Jack Black. That scene was similar to when I first met my friend's girlfriend. When he pointed her out amongst the crowd, that movie was all I could think of. My friend had to get up then proceed to walk her to our table. When he went out to escort her towards our table, I thought to myself, no way this is the girl my friend spoke so highly of. Now, I can be shallow sometimes myself, but I knew my friend very well. Considering things he had told me, this woman wasn't his cup of tea compared to women I had seen with him in the past. His girlfriend wasn't a bad-looking woman; she just couldn't be compared favorably to the type of woman I'd seen Mannie approach and date since I'd known him.

It was astonishing to see him with someone so different from himself. My friend is a straight-laced type of guy who would do anything to get your approval, especially if he thought you didn't like him. He's the type of guy who would shit bricks if you embarrassed him in public or drank too much and became belligerent. If you were on a bar patio and a sign on the building said, "No Smoking," and you pulled out a cigarette, Mannie would make sure he prevented you from smoking even if the sign meant "No Smoking inside the building." That is the type of guy he is. Yeah, he is that anal about things and very uptight. I remember a statement from the book *Unfu*k Yourself* by Gary John Bishop. He said that most people act out subconsciously to prove one of their parents didn't raise them right, when in actuality, they sometimes had very loving parents. That's why we drink too much or get on drugs. In my friend's case, I think that's the reason he had a deep, meaningful relationship with someone opposite of who his parents would never allow him to get married to.

When my friend and his girlfriend finally broke up, he was devastated. He had put all of his focus, time, money, and attention into his ex-girlfriend, trying desperately to get her approval to marry him. He even mentioned how he had good insurance to assist her with ongoing medical treatment for her back. I believe that's why they never married and why she ended the relationship. My friend did a lot of talking but barely showed how much he wanted to be with her. They had planned to move in together after her lease was up. My friend did not comment when the time came and ended up giving her an excuse of why he couldn't move in with her. The same thing happened when he talked to her about getting married. He never took the initiative to get an engagement ring to show his actions. Women want to see action because words mean nothing to them until you show them where you are coming from. It amazed me that a man with such status had no knowledge of being in a relationship. He seemed to be winging it half of the time. My friend has moved to the East Coast since then, his first time away from home as a man.

According to a book titled *Unscrewed Man,* written by Jeff Arnall, "The mindset a man needs to adopt through everyday life is Zero-Fucks Given." He says a man should train himself to not give a damn what other people think of him if he wants to be successful in life, especially when he is in a relationship or dating a woman. For example, you have to go on a date as if you are there to have a good time and not be in a relationship. No matter how attractive she is. A man should never want a woman more than she wants him. In my friend's case, he made being nice to her a priority; this is seen as a lack of self-worth. This is a psychological movement, and it all depends on your choices. If a woman doesn't give a damn about you, or perhaps she is always annoyed anytime she's around you, I would advise you to leave her and find another woman. There are better women out there who are much more attractive and fun to be with. I mean, natures differ, and the emotions and feelings you are going through might not be the same ones she is going through.

Chapter 8

Life When Married

I was in the military in my mid-twenties when I first got married. This was also the first time I lived away from home. I met a young, charming, vibrant, and attractive woman from the East Coast. Our meeting was unusual because I had no desire to be in a relationship after a horrible break-up with my last girlfriend of three years. When I met my wife, we were both in the military. She was one of the cooks and I would see her while going through the lunch line. She was so attractive that all the other guys in my unit couldn't take their eyes off of her but she would only flirt with me every time I went to the cafeteria.

One day, on my way to a house party, I ran into her. We started talking and ended up having long conversations about life and what we wanted to do when we got out of the military. It was the first time I had ever been turned on emotionally by a woman. After some time, we started dating and became boyfriend and girlfriend for two years before we decided to marry. I didn't know how nice of a guy I was back then, and I was with a needy and insecure woman. In a way, it made it easy for me to be with her in which her neediness complimented my nice guy persona. The issue that I had while being married was that I spent all my time trying to please her. In return, it often resulted in us arguing about her needs.

The fact is, you can never please a woman no matter how hard you try. You can only give a woman what she needs and not what she wants. Other times, you find yourself trying to please her in the hope of not creating conflict.

Because of my wife's neediness, I didn't allow my own purpose to come forth in the relationship. According to David Deida, the author of *The Way of the Superior Man*, "The next time you notice yourself giving in to your woman, postponing your mission, and denying your true purpose to spend time with her, stop. Tell your woman that you love her, but you cannot deny your heart's purpose." Your purpose must always be your focus. Giving too much attention to your woman will surely fail, and all your efforts to try to make her happy will fail. I didn't understand this when my marriage ended after two years of being together. My actions as a nice guy or Beta male had forced her to seek someone more masculine and less attentive than I. I know what you may be thinking to yourself, but unfortunately, society and watching too much television has misinformed us. What we have been taught about what women want isn't true. Even though a woman will say, "I want a man to give me attention..." when she gets it, she will lose all interest in you. That's why a man's priority must always come first.

Having something more important to focus on will allow your woman to see you as a masculine man who follows his goals. This is an attractive trait that women like to see in a man. A woman wants a man who is confident and outspoken. A woman wants a man who cares for what she wants and someone who can hold a conversation with her and keep her interested. When you believe in yourself, know what you want from life, and understand who you are, women will be attracted to you. Nevertheless, you need to understand that there is a difference between being confident and being an egomaniac. Mystery attracts women. They believe that there are many stories hidden from the rest of the world. They love the concept of discovering new things about their man over time. Women want to know the part of your life she doesn't get to see. They know that it takes someone special for you to reveal who you are, and they want to be that person. The more you try to hide your information from her, the closer she wants to come, and the more you try to cover, the more she wants to see. "Never chase love, affection, or attention. If it isn't given freely by another person, it isn't worth having." -Anonymous.

"I use to be a fucking Beta Male, now before you guys start thinking did you change your charisma, what happened? Did you lose some weight? Did you start making more money? Guys, I can't remember the exact age I became an Alpha Male. I think it was around the age of 27. But up to that point, I was a Beta- Male. Now what changed from me being a Beta-Male up to 27 from me being a pure Alpha-Male from 27 on over? What happened? Guys, the only thing that changed in that time. I'm the same guy, my personality is the same. My financial situation went up a bit. And obviously like everybody else my weight has fluctuated up and down. Some years I've been heavier than others but pretty much I'm the same guy. The only thing that's changed guys, primarily is my mindset."
- Alpha Male Strategies

Chapter 9
How to be an Alpha around Girls

The Alpha, by definition, is the leader of the pack. In the animal kingdom, the Alpha rules over the Beta Male and the Omega Male. In just about every environment that includes human society with the option to mate with every female within his territory. An Alpha will even travel amongst other territories of other Alpha Males. And if he is confronted by other Alphas he will show them a display of who is more dominant while trying to take over the other Alphas' territory. Once the new Alpha takes over the new territory, he will try to mate with all the females of his choice within that territory. The same is true when it comes to human society, although the dynamics are a little different compared to the animal kingdom. For example, if you're a Beta Male or Omega Male, you already know how quickly an Alpha Male type of guy can come along and take your job, your girlfriend you're your territory. When you really think about it, a lot of people don't believe the world works like this. But it's the reality that we live in. Think of it like this:

when you go into your job or office building or classroom, which guy in the room you would like to avoid? Or which family members at the family reunion do you do your best to keep your distance from and try not to deal with them if you don't have to? Which person in the classroom makes you cringe because of their aggressive attitude? That, my friend, is your Alpha Male. The strong, attractive, confident, masculine guy within your social circle. Even on the bus or on the streets there's an Alpha somewhere. He is the guy who talks to every pretty girl at the party or club and hooks up with them afterwards.

The truth is, life is much easier as an Alpha if you muster just enough courage within yourself to take more chances in your life. You can become an Alpha in any situation. The problem is, you're thinking about the consequences instead of seeing the results. Therefore, you're causing yourself to limit yourself to take action. The problem with this is a lot of guys don't know what an Alpha looks like in different parts of social cues. When the Alpha is amongst friends, the Alpa is constantly reaching for his full potential and shows greater emotional strength during the process. He has the ambition to achieve big goals in life. At the same time, the Alpha Male understands that you can't please everyone, and he doesn't try to. The Beta males and Omega males are always talking about their goals, but never take action on them. The Alpha is always moving forward and making progress toward his goals.

How can you be the Alpha around girls? This is a big problem for a lot of guys out there. Either you're the 40-year-old guy who still lives in his mother's basement or the 17-year-old who is still in school. Any man can become an Alpha, but you need to know how an Alpha acts when he's around girls. On a normal day, you may have seen average-looking guys with very attractive girls. It's either Facebook, Instagram or other social media platforms you have thought to yourself. How did he get her? He paid her to be on Instagram with him, it's no way he is hooking up with her. Or you've seen an average guy on your way to the mall who doesn't look like Brad Pitt but looks like Steve Buscemi who played Crazy Eyes from the Adam Sandler movie Mr. Deeds out with a very attractive woman. The first thing you think is, he must have money or a nice car. Not even close, what this guy has is confidence and he has realized that women need to become attracted to your personality first. Women don't necessarily look at appearances when finding a mate. That's why you will sometimes see a below-average guy with a very attractive woman. Because most women will rather be with a below-average guy over a highly good-looking guy. Unfortunately, a lot of these highly attractive guys are insecure, shy, and unsure of themselves. Even though they look like Brad Pitt or an Alpha they lack the confidence to carry themselves as such. Therefore, if you can display the traits of an Alpha when you're around women, you will be able to approach any woman you want and be amazed at how you will be treated by attractive women. The key is understanding how an Alpha behaves around attractive women. They are respectful amongst others, and treat everyone the same. Don't put her on a pedestal because she's attractive. At the same time, as the Alpha, you must stay confident, and calm under pressure regardless of how stressful the environment may be. Just imagine Daniel Craig as James Bond in the 007 movies, how calm and cool he is under every stressful situation, but still gets the job done without panicking. As such, the Alpha also makes the women around him feel feminine and comfortable because of the energy he puts out.

There is nothing more pleasurable to a woman than to be able to be feminine when she is around a man who brings it out of her. There's a great way to be aware of this, if you're around a woman and you feel like you're more of a woman or more of one of the girls when you're around her. This is a good indicator that you're putting out the wrong vibe to the women around you. When you're in the presence of other women they expect the man to take the lead, As the man you don't expect the girl to do it for you. As such, you as the man don't expect the woman to make a move first nor does he force it. In addition, if you want to be an Alpha around girls. You must be prepared for a woman's test.

A woman will test you even if you've just met her or are in the middle of a conversation with them. What she is doing when she tests you is she is testing your emotional strength. It's her way of trying to find out if you're really an Alpha. These tests will come in different ways, such as giving you the cold shoulder after meeting you, to see if you get discouraged. Another way a woman may test you is by teasing you or challenging your manhood. This can happen somewhere during the conversation to test your confidence. When this happens, a true Alpha will stay calm, cool, and collected when these tests are put in front of them. You shouldn't take it personally from a woman. When a woman does this, a lot of guys get discouraged and feel that she is being mean. In reality, she is only testing your masculinity and confidence. As an Alpha, you must understand this in order to become comfortable enough to be around attractive women. In conclusion, if you want to be more Alpha around women, start improving yourself such as going to the gym, learning to play sports, and facing your fears by being more social. These things will help assist you in doing your best to not be a Beta male nor an Omega Male around women. Even though we, as a society, don't want to admit it, the Alpha Male is the guy who gets the most rewards from life. He gets respect from others, most of the money, and most of the opportunities with women.

Conclusion

I hope this book gives you some insight into dealing with women and how to handle your relationships. When I first started dating, my parents had already divorced, and my mom had moved my sister and me halfway across the country from Miami, Fla, to Dallas, Tx. Since my dad lived so far away, my opportunities to learn how to date and meet girls as a young man were minimal. I came to believe that meeting women and having relationships with women could only be a struggle for me. I always ended up having hurt feelings and not understanding what I was doing wrong.

At first, I thought the lessons I learned from watching T.V. and chick-flick movies were the best way to treat a woman. It took me a long time to realize that those lessons weren't applicable when dealing with women in the real world. Even though a woman will say that she wants to be treated the way the men in movies treat women—such as bringing her flowers on the first date or buying her a gift after only knowing her for a week or two—I quickly discovered this wasn't true. These were all the wrong lessons. Acting in these ways only makes a woman find out how insecure and needy the man really is. For a woman, and her feminine emotions, it is a big turn-off. I watched these romance movies as a young man thinking it would help me stand out and show her that I was worth her time.

I learned the hard way. I was occasionally told "You're a nice guy, but..." and "Can we be friends?" In the long run, these experiences have taught me how dating and relationships really work. As a result, I would usually get kicked to the curb within a week, sometimes within a month in getting to know her. The reason why I'm telling you this is because I am hoping you are able to change the way you have been doing things when dealing with or dating women and being in a relationship. I realized there must be a better way for me to stop getting my feelings hurt. So, I started reading books about masculinity, chasing your purpose, being a man, books on making money, and dating women.

Ever since I started reading these types of books, things have drastically changed for me. Not just in my relationships and meeting women but also in my personal life and finances. I hope reading this book will help guide you in the right direction. Hopefully, learn from your mistakes and change your life to become a better man.

About The Author

Chris Finley is the author of **Alpha Male Mentality** and **Sigma Male Mentality**. He enjoys teaching people how to stay motivated and lead the lives of their dreams, passions, relationships, and businesses. He is a professional dating coach and a public speaker.

Do Not Go Yet; One Last Thing To Do

If you enjoyed this book or found it useful, I'd be very grateful if you'd post a short review. Your support does make a difference, and I read all the reviews personally to get your feedback and make this book even better.

Thanks again for your support!

References

Summers, Marc.2017. *How to Quit Being a Loser With Women: and Become the Man Women Instantly Want*. Independently published. 105.

Jones, Caleb. 2018. *The Unchained Man: The Alpha Male 2.0: Be More Happy, Make More Money, Get Better with Women.* Audiobook. DCS International, LLC

Bishop, Gary John. 2017. *Unfu*k Yourself* Audiobook. Harper One

Corey, Wayne. 2013. *How To Be A 3% Man, Winning The Heart Of The Woman Of Your Dreams. eBook.* 108